TEN THOUSAND SELVES

Ten Thousand Selves

POEMS

Chloe Martinez

THE WORD WORKS
WASHINGTON, D.C.

THE WORD WORKS
P.O. Box 42164
Washington, D.C. 20015
editor @ wordworksbooks.org

Author photograph: Kilian Kröll
Cover design: Susan Pearce Design
Cover Art: Woman riding composite horse.
Approx. 1800–1850. India: Thanjavur, Tamil Nadu state.
Opaque watercolors on paper.
Asian Art Museum of San Francisco,
Gift of Mr. and Mrs. George Hopper Fitch,
1988.51.6. Photograph © Asian Art Museum of San Francisco.

LCCN: 2021941571
ISBN: 978-1-944585-49-5

ACKNOWLEDGMENTS

Many thanks to the editors of the following publications, in which poems from this manuscript have appeared (some in slightly different forms):

The American Journal of Poetry: "Dürer's *Saint Jerome in His Study*" and "On the Train from Vienna to Budapest"

Another and Another: An Anthology from the Grind Daily Writing Series (Bull City Press): "The Mirror" and "The River Reed" (from "Four Past Lives, As I Recall Them")

Barzakh: "After Morning Drop-off I Change the Station"

Cagibi: "The New Mother Before the End Times"

The Collagist: "Zoomorphic"

The Common: "The God Structure"

Construction: "Microscopic"

The Cortland Review: "Babur at Agra"

Crab Orchard Review: "Sheep Meadow" and "First Night"

EcoTheo Review: "Bloom"

Exposition Review: "The Flower Vendors"

Faultline: "Villanelle" and "The Woman in Degas' *Women Ironing* Leans In"

Four Way Review: "The Mirror Room"

Gold Wake Live: "Aubade"

The Indianapolis Review: "The Jade Cicada" and "36 Text Messages, 16 Missed Calls"

Moist Poetry Journal: "Not-Yet-Official Girl Scout Badges" and "Seeing the Rare Douc Langur"

Negative Capability Press blog: "The Emperor Jehangir at Vah Garden"

The Night Heron Barks: "Display"

The Normal School: "Apollo" and "Ant Killer" (from "Four Past Lives, As I Recall Them")

PANK: "Inequality Poem"

Parentheses: "Natural History"

Penn Review: "Mandala of the Mountain Path" and "The Getaway"

The Potomac Review: "Palace Gate"

Prairie Schooner: "Mandala of the Soapy Water" and "Arrangements"
Relief: "At Red Bucket Equine Rescue"
Rise Up Review: "The Spinster at the Party"
RHINO: "The Movement"
Shenandoah: "Mandala of the Pile of Papers on the Dining Room Table,"
    "Study Finds," and "Motherhood: A Map"
SWWIM Every Day: "At the Nimbus Fish Hatchery" and "Seal Beach"
Waxwing: "Afterlife"

Some of these poems appeared in *Another and Another: An Anthology from the Grind Daily Writing Series* (Bull City Press, 2012), as well as in the chapbook *Corner Shrine* (Backbone Press, 2020).

For their support over the many years during which this book took shape, thanks to teachers, friends and colleagues at Barnard College, UC Santa Barbara, the Creative Writing Program at Boston University, the MFA for Writers at Warren Wilson College, Frost Place, Vermont Studio Center, and Claremont McKenna College.

To my family, friends, and all those whose community, feedback, and encouragement sustains me, so much love and thanks. Indebted to you always: Poetry Binders; the Grind; Leslie Blanco and the Lit Lunch writers; Angela Narciso Torres and the RHINO family; Courtney Thomas, Genevieve Kaplan and the poets of Claremont, CA; Lili Ibara; and Kate Hollander and Regan Huff of the No-Kill Poetry Shelter— one of the best things to come out of one of the worst years.

Deepest gratitude to everyone at The Word Works; special thanks to Susan Pearce for her patient and wonderful cover designing; but most of all to Nancy White for her joyful and wise editorial eye, ear, and heart.

For Jamel, Amina and Saafia.

For Michael.

CONTENTS

3

मण्डल [**mā́ṇḍala**] n. circular, round, a disc (esp. of the sun or moon); a circle (inst. 'in a circle;' also 'the charmed circle of a conjuror'), globe, orb, ring, circumference, ball, wheel; the path or orbit of a heavenly body… a round mole or mark (caused by a finger-nail etc.) on the body; a circular array of troops; a particular attitude in shooting; a district arrondissement, territory, province, country; …the circle of a king's near and distant neighbours (with whom he must maintain political and diplomatic relations); a multitude, group, band, collection, whole body, society, company… **mā́ṇḍala kavi**, m. a poet for the crowd, bad poet.

—Monier-Williams, *A Sanskrit-English Dictionary* (1899)

When you are free from everything that holds you back you can live in the world…

—*Therigatha* vs. 4 (6th-3rd c. BCE), trans. Hallisey

THE MIRROR ROOM

Mehrangarh Fort, Jodhpur, Rajasthan

You live in a high fort above a blue city. The rooftops below
speckled with laundry. At night the distant echoes
of a hundred brass bands, a hundred weddings. The blue
of the city is not quite robin's egg, not exactly
the blue of chicory. Outside the city is the desert.

Don't tell it like a story. It will sound too beautiful.
You stand on a high parapet, in the rustle and coo
of pigeons, under filigreed eaves. When you step over red
velvet ropes, leaving the museum behind, you find
rooms empty as the moon, floors carpeted in desert silt.

In one bedchamber-turned-cave, you hold your breath,
you bow before a rank hill of bat guano. You touch niches
for the ghosts of little lamps, and frescoed girls dance
with gods along the wall. Plaster dusts your fingertips.
Stained glass windows turn your thin skin rainbow. You take

a photo of a white hallway: Mughal arches echo, fade into
light. Not a story, not an image. It is a map. At the end
of the hallway, a balcony—the ground hazily distant—
the wide-winged turkey vultures gliding so close—hold
tight to the railing, notice how soft the sandstone carved

into curling vines. Notice it is crumbling. *Mehrangarh* means
Sun Citadel. *Sheesh Mahal* means Mirror Palace, or else
Hall of Mirrors, but it is just a tiny space, dim, claustrophobic
with reflections: wild, intimate room, it wants an audience.
Here you are, alone with your ten thousand selves.

1

LEARNING EXPERIENCE

I was traveling alone in India. I was an eighteen-year-old
idiot. When I fell from the moving train—the door

open, someone falling against me and then
my own fall, out of the door and onto the concrete

platform of Mathura Junction Station—I landed
hard, breaking my jaw and several teeth, the

crunch sounding inside my head, a sound
I would never forget. Years, later, when

someone asks me to write about a learning
experience, this is what comes to mind: the blue,

blue silence of the sky. The alarmed faces
of passers-by. The trains that kept on coming,

then going away. I sat bleeding on a bench
for a long time. A man gave me his handkerchief

and I held it against my face. Another man
handed me something—ah, it was my own tooth—

and walked away. And how lucky I was.
Even when I could not speak, no one put me

in a cage. Silent, enraged, I threw the tooth away
on the dirty tracks. Hoisted my bag with my one

free hand. Got myself on the next train home.

MANDALA OF THE PILE OF PAPERS
ON THE DINING ROOM TABLE

Star of pain in your neck: turn it side to side,
        it glows in the dark all the same. Your poster
                of the Golden Temple keeps falling down over your

desk, and the latest baby announcement watches you
        severely from the top of the pile, *send the gift already*,
                says the baby, so new it hasn't yet learned

how to smile. What is the proper order. How to
        master your materials. Annual reminder: *protect yourself*
                from the flu, and a catalogue full of things you hate

and also want. You try to imagine spending thousands on
        "The Lombok Bed," you stare at its hand-carved filigree, imported
                perhaps from its namesake island in Indonesia, site

of a recent earthquake (death toll: twenty). Made in China,
        more likely. The enormous headboard resembles a flower-
                mandala but, I kid you not, painted white, and no illusory

demons wait here for the boho-chic sleeper to encounter
        in dreams or visions. There will be no battle against the senses,
                no progress from the simple periphery to the inner circle,

which contains, in some traditions, the most fearsome opponents,
        some dangerously beautiful, others just plain dangerous. The catalogue
                bedroom is light-filled, tidy. A single houseplant hangs

from an exposed beam, and a small green bottle of San Pellegrino
      rests by the bedside. A room you float into, unencumbered by karma,
         by want, by messy piles of paper. Mandala: a universe map.

At its center, enlightenment, which is to say, freedom from
      causing harm. Move through it by touch, by starlight.
         Demons may appear. Persevere. Don't look them in the eye.

THE GETAWAY
Palm Springs

Sound puzzle, you cluck irritatingly on the living room floor
when left to your own devices, or stay silent when prompted,
or else you moo. Guilt gift from a trip on which I hardly had time

to touch a cactus. Mother-love, mother leaving, "girls' getaway"
weekend experiment. Poolside time fraught with
phone calls. My friends, the two Jennies, in their bright

sundresses, well, we did have a drink in one of those
Sinatra bars, something about the moon, full of rather joyful
possibly alcoholic retirees. By the morning I'm pacing around

the midcentury modern antique shop, the sun rising over the
fiberglass dinosaur off Route Ten as the Jennies consider
fiestaware and my clock runs out. You have learned new

grammatical constructions just to demand my immediate
return, all night. My breasts ache anyway, still trained to
produce for you, and still, there is nothing better than your anger

silenced by your hunger. Suck, suck, you eye me through your
long lashes. How much longer? Child, just wait until you
taste a little freedom. You'll always want more, and more.

DISPLAY

The tiger is hiding somewhere in his cage.

A sign says to watch out for rattlesnakes, but the only person here

is a peacock, alone at the end of the path, who decides

to stun me with beauty: the famous tail, almost

tragic in its weight, the bejeweled temptation

of its feathers—he gives it a shimmy-rustle and the layers

rise up just a little, expanding

like a lung. Then they lay back down. Then the real

thing, the full opening-out, the bird-body

as stage, curtain rising by invisible pulleys: when it reaches

full fan, he makes his turn, all three hundred and sixty

degrees of him, slow-sweep wall

of color, time-stopper, he shows me

his architecture and he does it with total

control, his elegant legs tensed to hold up those thousand

Indra-eyes. I'm still standing there, gaping, when he proceeds in my pitiful direction, the deep shining

blue of his chest preparing to crush me

like a wave, unapologetic, perfect

as the night sky: too close, impossibly far away.

BABUR AT AGRA

Then in that charmless and disorderly Hind, plots of garden were seen laid out…
—Baburnama (Memoirs of Babur), *trans. Beveridge*

Having conquered the subcontinent, the emperor
was lonely for the cool Afghani hills, the windy plains

of Mongolia, the hanging gardens of Kabul. So,
although he had palaces in Delhi, he told his architects

to make him proper gardens, planned in accordance
with the layout, as best they could estimate, of Paradise:

attention was paid to symmetry, to holy numbers,
and he requested cool baths, shade-giving trees,
and those flowers that fill the air with sweetness at night.

When it was done, the emperor's servants brought
a brocaded chaise, a carpet patterned with birds.

On hot afternoons he received guests in the shade
on the terrace nearest the river, to catch the breeze.

At night he walked the fragrant pathways,
thinking of when he slept in the open air.

SEEING THE RARE DOUC LANGUR IN THE SEMI-WILD

Outside Da Nang

In pictures: his round ruminant belly. He chews
betel leaves all day. Bright ochre legs, sensitive face, framed
with a white ruff. When blinking: mysterious blue eyelids.

*How do we protect it? We bring people. They see the monkey
and they fall in love.* Unburdened, confident, the eco-tour guide
took us up the mountain. Even the children grew quiet,

squinting into the leafy depths. Finally we stopped and gazed
into the douc's shining eyes, which remained quite open,
no blue to see but that of the sky. We stood in the empty road

clutching cameras. Meanwhile, the douc, regal,
plucked a branch and removed each one of its leaves,
just as I do with a bunch of basil.

His sharp little mouth moved, chewing.
The sea like a sparkling tray was held up
in the background of him. The red-shanked douc ignored it.

AFTER MORNING DROP-OFF I CHANGE THE STATION FROM KISS-FM TO THE KAVANAUGH HEARINGS

In the car we rewrite pop songs so that
Selena Gomez sings *I want to hold you*
in my mind enclosure and I
and my seven-year-old girl, we sing along.

The other day in despair I thought *maybe I should tell her*
now, before she'll need to know, how to fend off
the world, I mean eyes I mean words I mean
hands on her. My mind enclosure struggles
to even think this thought. But it's all over

the radio: girls and women only just now learning
words for what was done or almost done, for what had
undone them wordlessly. I want her to have words.
I want nothing done to her. I want for her
an entirely different language. The time I went with a friend

to some lame grad student party: suburban ranch house,
my first week in a new town, people standing around.
Halfway through my one drink, I was
encased in my own body, mummified awake,
could not speak, could barely walk. I was lucky.
My friend hauled me home to sleep it off. I never
went there again. Filed no complaint with any
authority, advisor, safe human. Because nothing

happened, didn't it? Did it? All my eloquent
application essays, my conference talk, my study
of five languages, gave me no words for
that. You're okay. Move along, file away.

To tell her these things is to
darken her whole world. To not tell her
invites lyrics that can't be
rewritten, forgotten, misheard.

NATURAL HISTORY

They've been dead for decades, since long before I was born.
My mother saw them on school trips: two white wolves

caught mid-leap, suspended in eternal blue twilight,
endless arctic summer. I stand just where I can see

the darkness inside their panting mouths, the empty air
between their front feet and the unbroken crust

of snow—they haven't landed on it yet, though they throw
their shadows ahead of them. It's almost inevitable

that the tail of the left one will graze that
low-hanging branch, and a few wet clumps of snow will

shower down as they pass. The painted Northern Lights,
the flat horizon-line they run to. I am eight, watching them,

and nineteen, and forty: the silent velocity of their feet,
of my heartbeat in the dark, the pockmark

panic of rabbit tracks before them in snow.

36 TEXT MESSAGES, 16 MISSED CALLS

Fifty strangers are trying to reach me. They all want to know
about seven boxes of laminate that someone—not me—
is giving away on Craigslist. The flooring is somewhere

in Sacramento. They leave me their contact info.
The inquiries range from casual—"Heyyyy my name's
Jose do you still have the boxes"—to formal: "Good evening,

I am interested in the flooring …" Some of them take
a pleading tone—"if you still have the flooring, I'll come
and get it right now ???" One person says, "I need flooring

desperately!" A lady named Dee writes a warm message
signed, "Thank you very much." Linda writes twice. Ed seems
pretty chill: "I can take those off your hands." They are in

Fair Oaks, Folsom, Citrus Heights. They are ready
to come and get all seven boxes of laminate flooring
tomorrow morning, tonight, right now. They've been ready

since yesterday, and they don't know why they haven't yet
heard back from me. They are friendly, cordial, they have learned
my name from my voicemail greeting, so they say, "Hi Chloe!

Hi Carly! Hello Cleo! Hey, Cole." I can hear Cassandra's
kids in the background. Everyone so full of hope.
Everyone thanking me in advance. On Craigslist Sacramento,

I find my listing. I ask the person who really is
offering all that flooring for free to please,
please correct the phone number, so that at least one

of these fifty-two people (so far), of whom I've become
quite fond, even protective, might be able to have
what they wish for: gleaming new floors. May we all

catch a little free beauty sometimes. May at least one
of our earnest, desperate, hopeful calls be rewarded
with bounty. With gifts unearned and earned. With free

laminate flooring, enough to make one room, at least, like new.

ARRANGEMENTS

Because the lilies aren't ready to bloom
the women of the wedding party fan out

across the reception hall, lean close
to each cluster of green and with two fingers

unlock the petals from one another,
nudge them apart enough to let light

slip in—flowers don't know what moves them,
they find themselves falling open,

one after another imperceptibly slow explosion,
awake, *awake*, they cry silently,

all around them the silverware
in formation, the wide-open faces of plates, expectant

white expanses of tablecloth, quiet now,
for the women have gone to pin white jasmine

in their hair, and the men pace on the lawn
in Sunday suits, squinting upwards,

reading the sky for signs of rain.

MANDALA OF THE NATURE CENTER SLEEPOVER

There is pizza. The fish that ignored us during the day
  now seem to take an interest. Maybe we imagine it.
    The sea horses are holding hands with their curly tails.

There is one small octopus asleep in a rock-cave,
  eye closed, mysterious heart-engine pumping visibly.
    There is a craft project. A scavenger hunt.

The children and their adults wander back and forth,
  the moray eel opening and shutting his mouth
    in a terrifying corner, and then we notice the octopus

has awakened. She curls and uncurls, tentacle-cakewalks
  across the glass wall, then rockets herself through the water,
    and the way she moves doesn't say *escape* or *hunger*,

though once we see her false eye-spots glow
  bright blue as if (her label says) under threat,
    but that color fades, and she goes on far beyond easy

explanations: a dance of being alive in a body,
  a dance of the body alive. The octopus is
    unlike us. The octopus is more like us than we

can explain. What I mean is, the multiplicity
  of her suction cups! Unimaginable! And yet
    right here before our eyes, the truth: beauty.

We stand in a semi-circle before her tank,
  watching for as long as the octopus chooses to move
    us. We stay quite still. Fallen silent. Seen.

THE SPINSTER AT THE PARTY

As a child you assume the world exists
only as you enter rooms, but recently

you've found the disdain of the powerful
so tiring, so enraging, actually, that you've begun to imagine

becoming enormous, like the palm tree
you sometimes pass when driving

to the dentist: the trunk goes up, then turns
sideways, nose-dives down to the ground—

At a work thing you sit with a circle of men,
and your colleague says loudly, *Hey, now a woman is here!*

She must be the spinster at the party! Which doesn't
even make sense, you're married. At another work thing

an old man joins your table for lunch,
a table full of women. He announces to the women at the table,

It's like a quilting bee in here!
The women stare at him in silence, concentrating

on the palm tree's trunk, how it keeps on growing
horizontally, then just at a slight incline.

AT THE NIMBUS FISH HATCHERY
Sacramento

Nimbus: droplets in air, cloud-thought word
that rainbows at the right angle, as along

       the stair-step artificial river where the rainbow
       trout start small, just gently making their way

upstream—but if we proceed to the first little
waterfall place, we see the bigger ones making

       the leap, some failing and one caught mid-
       evolution for a moment, gripping with one fin-

arm the tiny fence, falling back—but they keep
flinging forward their slick slight bodies, as if trying

       to demonstrate a principle, as if God made them
       to show us what effort is. A real river is rushing,

after recent rains, beside us, but the rainbows
don't even know or care, or do they? But at the top

       of the fake stream, the wall is higher, so
       the biggest fish leap up again and again but cannot

cross over—but the breathless curl of their
fan tails, but the wild and doomed enterprise of them—

       but we lean forward, watching, as if our bodies
       might lift theirs into the air, but a little higher—

STUDY FINDS

Study Finds One in Eight Men Think They Could Score
a Point off of Serena Williams. Study finds 13% of boys pretend

expertise; the word the study uses is "bullshit." Men Speak
92% of Time on Company Conference Calls, Study Finds. Study finds

male scholars are more likely than female scholars,
across disciplines, to engage in self-

citation. Study finds that men speak twice as often as women do
at colloquiums, a difference that can't be explained away

by rank, speaker pool composition or women's interest
in giving talks. Study Finds Men Who Hold Traditional Views of Women

Earn More Than Men Who Don't. New Study Shows That Men
Are Twice More Likely Than Women to Believe

There Is Equal Gender Fairness in the Workplace. Study
Finds Men Want to Help Women at Work, But Just Don't Know

How. Married Women Do More Housework than Single Moms, Study Finds.
Study Finds Men Are More Afraid of Bugs than Women.

Study Finds Men Funnier than Women. More than 90%
of Grammy nominees are men, USC study finds.

For Online Daters, Women Peak at 18 While Men Peak
at 50, Study Finds. A Harvard Study Finds that Men are 5

Times More Believable than Women. Alligators have "taste" for Florida men, study finds.

Women are diagnosed years later than men for same diseases, study finds. Use of Male Mice Skews

Drug Research Against Women, Study Finds. Penn Study Finds Men Are More Likely To Receive

CPR in Public than Women. Drivers crowd women on bikes more often than men, study finds. Nearly 2,000 Women

Murdered by Men in One Year, New Study Finds.

BOX MAKING

A book begins with planned proportions too:
the corners squared, flat covers sheltering flat pages—
but in time it grows soft, crooked, the spine
broken, one marbled endpaper peeling up.
Left out in the grass on a summer night,
the pages swell and soften, rippling.

Take its measurements. From these, calculate
the shape the box will take, adding
allowances for overlaps, folds.
Two long rectangles fit together like a paper angel.
An awl inflicts two holes for rivets, two more
where strings will go to hold it closed.

It is a kind of ending, this act of preservation,
and everything resists: a quiver of the wrist
and the box comes out glued crooked, or with a fold
too close to let it close.
The board strains against its ties
and wants to warp: it holds the memory of trees.

KERALA

Here is a sidewalk made of stones balanced
like children's blocks: some have shifted or

fallen in, revealing what's under them: air,
and sometimes a trickle of water. Here

is the heat of the day. Here is the problem of how to step
across these spaces, whether this one that slants up

will support us or not. Here is a movement
at the edge of our field of vision—let it not be

cockroach. Let it be leaf, candy wrapper, nothing, o
let us take note of the palm trees instead, look up! They are

everywhere. Here, crisscrossing the ground,
are their shadows: we walk over them as one walks

on a crosswalk, black-white-black-white-black—but let us
keep moving, do not be distracted by the gutter and its

coconuts. You must be thinking, coconuts, here
for the taking! The perfect food, it heals you

from the heat, from your exhaustion, it is meat
and water and oil all at once, it enriches a curry

and silkens your hair. It is a rough impenetrable
skull of a thing. You must be thinking, how does one

open a coconut, anyway? Well, here are men
with machetes who do that, they can chop one open

easily, and hand it to you with a pink plastic straw
for a few rupees. Take heart. Sit down here. Drink.

FOUR PAST LIVES, AS I RECALL THEM

The Thief

You were a tapestry
woven by medieval geniuses.

Fortified towns and castles were contained
merely in the background of you,

and all your flowers were real, each
identifiable by its Latin name—

had Latin names even been
invented in your time? Anyway,

I was a thief
who spent hours unraveling

only your gold and silver threads. Please
understand: I didn't want to do it, but

you sparkled so, and in those days
there was a war on, and I was always hungry.

The Ant-Killer

You were five hundred ants,
a black column winding across the kitchen wall,

pooling like ink in the trash can, if ink
were alive. You were looking for water, as you

(or some other five hundred ants)
always do in the heat, in September.

I was the woman
with the spray-bottle of Windex, I'm sorry,

in the middle of the night; five hundred
black specks, you, scattered in a panic;

subsided; died. The bottle leaked somehow,
bleach-smell strong on my hand for hours.

I was ruthless. I left all your dead bodies
stuck to the wall for the new scouts to find.

The River Reed

You were the calligrapher
whose job it was to copy

texts precisely, gracefully,
each letter distinct, a blade of grass.

I was a reed
growing on a riverbank. You came

absent-mindedly with a knife and
cut me into a shape you could use.

The Mirror

You were sleep, and
I was summer rain.

You were the notebook
lying open on the red couch
so that one of your pages
lifted, fell, lifted in a
current of air, and
I was gravity,
just barely keeping you there.

You were a painting
leaning against an empty fireplace, and
I was the threat—slight,
but present all the same—of fire.

You were shadows
cast by a ceiling fan that
turned just fast enough to
move the air.
I was a mirror
on the wall over the fireplace;
you turned in me too.

You weren't the white wallpaper.
You weren't the fleur-de-lis.
You weren't the growl of empty stomachs.
I was not the television.

You were sleep, and
I was the darkness
in which you came running.

2

BABY GRAND

Impractical beauty! It takes up too much space
and time, and it's so heavy, I mean—it just

crushes every modern notion
of efficiency, of "smart design," of the minimal. It fills
the place. It is more than five feet long.

Where you expect three legs, it has six.
The long piece of wood above the keys

is missing, so, seated, you see straight through
into its whale belly. It arrives on my 41st birthday,
a dark wooden curved piece of the nineteenth century,

somewhat scratched, containing a number of hairs
from a very long-haired cat. But it works.

I've been dreaming of it these many years.
Elegance of my teenage fingers
gone, and my curves thicker than I remembered too.

I wait, impatient, for my family to go out.
I'll begin again with scales. One hand, then two.

THE GOD STRUCTURE

It has a god structure. I think it will resist a long time.
—Customer review of the Uniqlo Beauty Light bra, $19.99

O keep me up, keep me going. Keep it together. Smooth me. Reduce
excess movement. There is a heaviness. There is around me
a God Structure. It helps me organize my thoughts. It has laid out
plans, I think, for various eventualities, and the existence of plans,

though they change, is a comfort. This morning the God Structure
led me to a vine that was drooping over the far edge
of the front lawn, covered with ripe blackberries. God Structure said,
Eat them, and I did. The stain of them still on my hands when I heard

that the God Structure had also made a disease that is suddenly taking
from my friend his body, among other things. It seems the God Structure
doesn't give a shit, has no alternate plan. Keep Google-ing it, nothing
appears. His tongue tries to choke him in his sleep. His God Structure

is written into his code: it was always there, in silence, inevitable.
Whatever has a God Structure is real. Is irresistible. Its tiny ticking
bricks, its termite-riddled beams, picturesque and stupid.
And also vast avenues that shape the light, and the sea that makes us

go on somehow, after we look at it, and also flying buttresses
that carry that weight, moving it outward, outward until it becomes
bearable. The God Structure has no need of metal underwire, it lifts
with mere stitches and foam, *beauty light*, it won't hoist me

too high, will it? God Structure, maybe you don't listen, but if by chance
you do: I could use just enough support to keep my tired
breast in its hapless place, awaiting plans, awaiting some revelation.
We speak on the phone, my friend's murderous tongue and me.

We say, at the end of the conversation, *I'll let you go*. The God Structure
has written us this script. We read it aloud. We hope to resist a long time.

INDRA SWALLOWTAIL
(Papilio indra)

…we ask Indra for help from here, or from heaven,
or from above the earth, or from the great sky.
—Ṛg Veda *1.6.10, trans. Müller*

Orange trees in the driveway

                                        in bloom, orange blossom perfume

heavy as the sunlight, and the black

                                        butterflies named after

the god of rainstorms

                                        are feasting, so many

you can hear their wings

                                        thunder-fluttering as you stand

close among them, after

                                        so many days

indoors

SEAL BEACH

A wave slides slantways under surfers, skinny teenage
hips kicked out as they fall in water
that swirls like mercury, and the kids
shrieking in the shallows, and the tankers

still as the corpses of giants along the horizon line,
and the pier rough-tumbling out to its conclusion.
Small boys: kick water at one other.
Old people: sit on the bench. Observe.

Skinny girls: selfie, selfie, text. My baby,
not a baby anymore, tugs my shirt aside anyway, nurses.
The surfers falling and falling. The first-grader's current
joke: Why do seagulls fly over the sea? Because,

if they flew over the bay they'd be bagels!
Bend the knees, bend the knees,
swivel-twist, fall back, fall back, fall.
A teen with boy-band bleached hair

smokes beneath the pier. You've been at sea
for some time now. You've been
sick of it. But then, the roar of the waves
calms you too. The kids are doing handstands

at the waterline like your inverted
brain, sand-suck around their hands
as the tide runs out, the world
upside-down, then slowly righting itself.

MANDALA OF THE MOUNTAIN PATH

The monk goes to bed early, rises pre-dawn, his robes
identical to other monks' robes, his routine fixed
and spacious: meditate. Study. Consume a small meal,

perhaps, and rest. The monk is not sharing his bed
with a preschooler who is fully potty-trained this week,
I hope. My in-laws went to Tibet, brought us back

a framed photograph of the Potala Palace. It hangs
in the bathroom: the impossible Himalayan peaks, the sharp
whitewashed walls, the garlands of stairways leading up

to another world. The monk sits on cushions on the floor,
his posture and breath perfected over time. He need not
squeeze in a mammogram before daycare pickup. His mind

is clear. I imagine it that way, anyway. Nothing against
the monk. His path is hardly an easy one. The icy
air up there; the leader in exile; the palace

turned museum; the yellow silk robe with its empty
sleeves folded on the golden throne. But sometimes
I am thinking a thought and then my husband and children

all shout at once: they have misplaced the things they need
right now and only I can find them. Nothing for it. No way
to be good enough, to make much progress through

the triple world. The dishes always waiting to be washed
though I hardly even cook: my husband cooks and cooks.
The dishwasher is small. Load it like someone climbing

a steep path, each dish placed gingerly all the way up
to the top—the round dome of the temple, the spinning
prayer wheel, the clean wind whipping the bright flags ragged.

VILLANELLE

"Let's write something…villanelles?" my friend said, and I said
"YES," and thought, *I could do that, just put the pieces*
together in a pattern…I wanted to make myself a bed

of words on which to lay my frantic head,
"I could do that," I said to myself in the car, *repeat,*
affirm, drive home, downshift on the curves, and invented

another me with the radio on, a little breeze—instead
I found myself in the kitchen again, my two sweet
daughters having blanketed the house with hundreds of red

and blue and grey and orange and pink small scattered
plastic things—I'm at the microwave. The small one's speaking
mysteries: "Brains? Or bones?" she says again and again

with a forkful of pasta, grinning. The large one's spread
eagle-ish on the couch, behind a book just her skinny knees
visible. What was it I meant to do or rather intended

to become? "Brains," my daughter says. "Bones." Bread
is rising somewhere. Shift gears, watch out for peace
which might be around that corner, right? We said
we'd make something. Pass it back and forth. Move ahead.

VETERANS DAY

I only want my hands to be like water: all day Debussy
runs through my head, "Doctor Gradus ad Parnassum,"
not plodding the way I play it, but liquid as in my dreams.

I don't know how to honor the dead. I don't trust
governments much. I remember both Dachau and Manzanar.

I want a clean, rippling sound. My mother once played
a corpse in a protest, her small slim body borne
through New York, flower-crowned in a box.

A blue-sky, windy day. I take my children
over to the empty elementary school playground.

They balance all the way, their bike-shadows
following them dutifully. They corkscrew
down the jungle gym, ignoring the pair

of blackbirds overhead who circle wildly,
chasing a hawk from their nest. For an hour

life seems almost comprehensible, progresses
nearly slowly enough for me to see its shape.
In truth, it hurtles ahead. In truth, we live in a country

where soldiers come home from war to stand guard
over kids in cages. "Doctor Gradus": first piece

in the *Children's Corner* suite. The last is "Golliwogg's
Cakewalk," which is jubilant and funny, which is named
for a doll based on blackface. It's so catchy, I can't get it

out of my American head. I only want to love
my country. I only want my hands to be like water.

INEQUALITY POEM

When you are exiled by circumstance, only the exile
is legible to others: your body, your illness, your employment

status, your poverty, your citizenship or lack thereof.
It is silently assumed of you that your exile must

have some reasonable cause, just as it is silently assumed
of the world that it is a fair and reasonable place

by those who have no experience of the alternative.
Let me put it another way: you are up in a tree,

leaves and the strength of your own limbs all around you
and the view is of rolling hills and insignificant

other people out enjoying a summer's day.
Their brightly colored clothes, their picnic blankets.

But what if you are up in a tree and down below you
is nothing but rushing water, and it is rising,

and the view is empty of people, others already
washed away, those who could not climb up

the tree, or were not near a tree, or who went back
to help a child, or whose tree branch broke beneath them?

This can no longer be, of course, a metaphor, and yet
it also still functions as metaphor. Isn't that something?

When you are exiled by circumstance, you become one
who knows that the world is a field of rising water,

that safety is the purview of the lucky, the able, the ruthless,
the unattached and the well-supported. You know the truth:

you are in the water scrambling for some solid ground,
or you are in the tree, or else you are already gone.

THE MOVEMENT

To human observers, the painted ladies move with speed and intention, as if
they have somewhere to be. They can fly as fast as 25 miles per hour.
—"Mass Migration of Painted Lady Butterflies Entrances
Californians," the *New York Times*, March 17, 2019

The painted ladies come through moving
in waves, little fluttering rivulets cutting
through the river delta of the sky, not a cloud, not exactly

a shadow, not a straight line among them and yet
a definite direction. You stand in the middle
of the space between buildings, your takeaway

lunch container in one hand and in the other, the idea
of progress, the temporary understanding
that there could be a distinct and also unified

movement towards. The sky is an electric
shade of blue. The truth is, they won't make it.
Not all, not the whole way—so along the route

they lay eggs, lay down, end.
Hatching later, new beings pick up
an invisible thread and just

continue, as if their parents' deaths were a mere
rest stop along the way.
Which, apparently, they were. Don't

cry: you are at your place of employment.
Make your way to privacy. Because you are
human, only there may you be moved.

THE LAST SYNAGOGUE IN ALEXANDRIA

An old man stared at us through the wrought-iron gate
and asked, "Jewish?" Yes, I said, But not my husband.

He checked our passports. "Stand in the shade!" he ordered,
so we stood in the shadow of the old synagogue, elegant

and empty in its gated grounds, its gardens. An even older woman
came along speaking French, hunched, black-skirted, bright-eyed,

looking us over. Ahead of us on the stairs she gripped the rail,
panting on the third step, "The sugar, how do you say? Diabetic!"

Inside, cool wooden benches, pink granite columns. She sat
in the front row while we wandered—"*Wander!*" she said—

under hanging lamps, high round windows. Who comes here?
we asked her. "Sometimes," she said, palms raised helplessly,

"many come, other times, none. Only three men are left
among us here, and five women." When we were done

I gave her ten Egyptian pounds. "I'll put it right here!" she said,
and tucked it in her shirt, beside her left breast, and laughed.

"Your husband, he is Muslim?" she said to me as we left.
"Well, all the religions, they are the same, no?" We nodded

and shuffled out past two dogs inert in the heat. The high gate
chained again behind us, we walked to the Corniche and looked

at the sparkling sea. There were the blind fishing-boats
with their painted Cleopatra-eyes, their patience as endless

as their loneliness. When the wind blew, they turned together
in silence and watched the horizon for some omen, some sign.

AUBADE

Barely-standing   in the sticky kitchen

the earliest part   of the morning, before even

coffee has really   woken up. You and I clutch

hot mugs, survey   the chaos: lunches

unmade; somehow   on the floor again

seven discarded   socks; the kids

rioting somewhere   upstairs.

The day waits   languid

as an unpaid bill.   A toast: to Tuesday.

Take a steaming   sip. Lean in and just

brush surfaces;   it is good to know

we still can, good   to scrape your stubble

and wake up. Here's   to pretending we can

miss the bus. To   two lovely minutes.

DÜRER'S *SAINT JEROME IN HIS STUDY*
From the 1514 engraving, Metropolitan Museum of Art

Translator hunched, haloed, slant
of light, bottleglass windows lining
the casements with little sun-targets
and a skull beneath them, and Christ
tiny on his desktop cross, and along
the back wall, each thing in its place:

scissors, sunhat, time in the hourglass,
rosary on a hook, and one enormous
gourd suspended on a rope from the ceiling,
calligraphy of drying vines. The lion and dog
repose in the foreground. The trestles
of his worktable: etched in all their specific

solidity, their shadows at rest on the floor.
His face bowed, of course, over the Book.
A man obsessed. Expert ascetic, patron saint
of translators. He took the thorn from the lion's paw.
His peace made by violence, a thousand
minuscule canyons cut into a copper plate,

Jerome at his work feels not the weight
of our eyes upon him. He is looking for the right
word. His name means *sacred name*. He had
a wicked temper. Relocated, late in life,
to a *spelunke* or cave, but Dürer gave him, instead,
this wood-beamed, sunlit, quiet room. *Sacred*,

cognate with *sacrifice*. *Room*, with *rural*,
roam, and also *ragged*, *ruin*. A setting-apart also
a desecration. An open space runs to desert.
Behind him, the silent progress of sun
and shadow on the wall. The dog, dreaming, smiles
in his sleep, and the lion stretches his tender paw.

ON THE TRAIN FROM VIENNA TO BUDAPEST

*There is no document of civilization that is not at the same time
a document of barbarism.*
—Walter Benjamin

Bags stowed over and under our seats, croissants
from the station unwrapped, devoured, and finally swept
neatly into the trash, we settle in

to stare out the window, Amina climbing
on each of us in turn, of course not sleeping,
and as we leave Vienna, then Austria behind us

and fields are interspersed with blocky buildings
and power lines, I can't help thinking *prison
tower labor camp* though I don't know

if there was one anywhere near here. In between,
lone figures show up bright and picturesque:
teenager in orange t-shirt and blue skirt

roller-skating down a dusty street; a guy asleep
by the side of the road, guardrail for his headboard;
an old man picking fruit from a tree; a woman

ascending a stairway. Amina hands me a sticky
half-eaten banana. The baby kicks inside me.
Uncle Kilian dozes. Jamel inspects the guidebook.

We pass a train loaded up with army tanks,
another with shiny new Audis. O O O O
say their logos. I am not one to keep on

resurrecting the past. How tiring the past is.
But today my mind keeps interrupting me
with *stripes bricks trains starvation*. The baby does her

flip-flop inside me and all's well. All all all is
well, I repeat to the empty train platforms, to the girl
making her way heavily down the street

on those old-fashioned skates. Her blazing yellow shirt.
her slight arms swinging wildly to keep her upright.

MANDALA OF THE REDWOOD FOREST
Sequoia sempervirens

Forest of trees whose name means Living Forever,

Softening the Ground, Gathering in Circles. They speak

in hushed tones over our little heads. Please stay

on the path, i.e., don't be that asshole over there

with her hippie hair, climbing on roots

two thousand years old, trying to get a better self-

ie. A tree-cave is hokey, isn't it? Well, who cares

if it is. Everyone waits for it. Everyone in turn

turns their phone to "flashlight," bends down,

creeps into belly of the whale: soft, smooth, in the flash

light slightly iridescent. A mothwing giant.

Everyone looks up to see or rather not see a perfect

upward arrow of space rising into darkness.

The temptation now to i.e. turn off the light.

PALACE GATE

Jodhpur, Rajasthan

The hand-prints of the sixteen *satīs* are carved in the wall,
colored with red powder (because they were wives), and gold

(for the fire). No, that's not true, red for auspiciousness and
gold for royalty. Red and gold for the colors brides wear. Red

the meat flung off the parapets in the golden dusk to feed
the huge circling kites, to prevent misfortune. Red a ring I stole

from a gift shop in high school. I still wear the ring,
and on my other hand, one band in plain gold, another with three

red rubies. Gold the field of daffodils where my mother
and sister and I were chased out by barking dogs,

red their collars. We thought it would be all right to pick them.
Red the Toyota hatchback that broke after so many years. Gold

the sedan that somebody gave us, that smelled always like
grandparents. Red my blood on the train platform, gold the dirt

on my knees, on my bleeding palms. Red the telephone, but
the shopkeeper had no phonebook. I wept on the counter; a gold

Ganesha looked on from his corner shrine. Red the sandstone palace,
even under whitewash. I never stole anything else.

THE FLOWER VENDORS

Unfinished fresco. Alfred Ramos Martinez, 1946.
Margaret Fowler Memorial Garden, Scripps College.

The baby caterwauls, who knows why. You snap
at husband, growl at kitchen mess, can't think of who
to complain to about your lucky life. Complain

to the mountains, then, they don't judge, they have actual
snow shining on their heads, and you can see them from this little
street where it never snows. It's almost cold.

Wrangle her into the tiny coat et cetera. Grab the notebook
and two books you won't get to read. Carry them like charms like a memory
of freedom. Get out out out among the sky and the winter citrus alive

yellow on the trees, push the stroller past the construction workers
who step aside and even attempt to wave their cigarette smoke
away as you pass. By the time you reach the secret walled garden

she is asleep. Two bubbling fountains. Piles of wisteria.
Along one wall the mural you came for: the women
like Amazon queens, hauling huge baskets of flowers on their backs

and balanced on their heads: zinnia and hibiscus and armfuls
of white calla lilies, and corn, and fruit, and aloe leaves like spears.
The trumpets of *floripondio* blossoms dangle behind them,

sweet-scented, heavy. Don't eat their seeds, for though hallucinogenic,
they can be fatal. The woman at the center wears a crown
of her own braided hair and stares out over your whole life.

Sit where she can see you. Breathe. Watch the green leaves and the bright blue sky
peter out at the end of the wall, the part left uncolored when the artist
died young: umber sketches of desert hills, outlined armadillo

and coyote lurking among them. The women with their long black braids
have a powerful quiet about them. Their eyes like almonds, their hands
monumental and strong. Martinez came to California for his daughter,

Maria, born with a bone disease, a warm, dry climate prescribed
by the best doctors he could find. She grew into health here, and he
did his greatest work, painting prayers of recovery for her:

Madonnas with their round babies, mythic Mexican goddesses,
La Malinche who either helped or betrayed her people (enslaved,
gifted to Cortés, interpreter of his conquests, bearer of his child).

Martinez painted women on the walls of chapels, hotels, cafes,
Beverly Hills mansions, and this garden that echoes Eden.
In this way father and child saved and raised each other.

Your baby keeps sleeping, lulled by the sound
of moving water. What you would not do to keep her
in this world. What worlds you would not keep making

for her survival and your own, even to the point of leaving them
unfinished. You cannot imagine. You can. You are sitting among
undone umber hills, growing cold. Red squirrels hurl themselves

through the loaded lemon trees. Look up. You are inside a walled
patch of sky, really. The blue is framed to show you its value.

ALMANAC

One minute, we were sitting in the many-windowed hall
listening to a lecture on George Herbert;
the next, snow flying behind every pane.
If today were an acrostic, it would read, amaze.

One minute, snowflakes melting on my hat;
the next, dark branches dipping under the wet
weight of crystals, sun shining through
in confusion, bright blue pieces of sky—

I had forgotten there could be seasons;
then you and summer arrived blazing green.
One minute, a small hunger-pang; the next, blackberries
shining among the thorns beside the road.

3

MANDALA OF THE SOAPY WATER

A few photos: sharp cheekbones, deep-set eyes, bequeathed
to his son, my father. Grandma remarried, erased him
so thoroughly he turned into smoke-rings, turned into

a stock story she told: *went out for cigarettes one day…*
and drifted away. My father, fathered by a cloud, became
a painter, someone who could turn anything beautiful.

Martinez our name, our mystery, mispronounced by me
until college. Then the apologetic *MAR*tin in my mouth,
the *ez* tacked on quietly, as if to escape notice, was corrected.

Over and over Mar*TIN*ez came back to me, the only way
New Yorkers knew how to say it. So his name, at least,
returned. Later, I searched databases for him. No trace. As if he never

was in the first place. Where a story of him would go is the sentence,
He was a dishwasher—that odd formulation, as if it were
a vocation, instead of a poorly-paid, backbreaking job

that he must have hoped to trade for something better.
Instead of a story, the vague notion that he was Puerto Rican.
Or "mixed": a little Spanish and Irish too. No story of who

his people were. The story is that he disappeared, but
no story is told of where he went, or why, or what happened to him.
He simply fades from family memory, in the murky middle of the 1950's.

Families gather around something, telling stories. What is there
at the center? Ring of smoke. In the absence of story, image:
soapy water, the white moons of plates coming up for air, sinking again.

Late night, hot restaurant kitchen, summer in the city. His rumpled white
apron, wet against the clank and spray of the sink. His sore back. His shining
soapy arms, circling. Ancestor. I want to imagine you another life.

FIRST NIGHT
New Bedford, MA

What a strange way of life
My heart maintains;
It lives in a lost way…
> —Amália Rodrigues, "Estranha Forma de Vida"

On the street, young men with blowtorches
carve huge blocks of ice into birds.

Standing at the front of the church,
a black lace shawl tied over her black dress,

she looks like any middle-aged woman
until she raises her head to sing

in the old sorrowing tradition, *fado*,
which means *destiny*, means *fate*,

means *lost at sea*, means *the nets came up
empty, all empty again.* New Year's Eve

in a city of lost nineteenth-century glories,
the city of my childhood, of fireworks seen

from the back porch in blankets and pajamas,
the explosions visible only through

bare trees in winter. That's all
gone now, and I don't even know

Portuguese, but I believed her when she
brought herself to tears, just a few at the end.

SHEEP MEADOW

Central Park, 1999

In the shade at the southern edge, you pause for a minute:
that green, that sunshine, extending ahead, ahead,
it sort of knocks the wind right out of you
to suddenly be in such a space, and there

is the old Russian, making balsawood glider-planes
with nothing but a knife, and giving them all away
to kids who toss them inexpertly up, then watch—
and you watch too—as they catch a current of air

and rise high above the trees, beside the skyscrapers,
becoming indistinct against the bright summer sky,
our eyes watering with the effort of keeping track
of where they go, until they're indistinguishable

from real planes, until they fade into blue, into memory.
He builds them perfectly. They never come down.

AT RED BUCKET EQUINE RESCUE
Chino Hills, CA

The heart is the smaller cousin of the sun. —Joy Harjo

Maybe your horse-heart was abandoned some time ago.

Maybe it was beaten with a broomstick or left to whittle itself
down in hunger to a set of ribs, rolling under a dull coat.

Even our history of violence may be redeemable. The heart waits,
hot, dusty, and barely breathing.
                           Go with a bucket.

Wash the heart gently, feed it up; it will in time grow
sleek and healthy again. If it fears you, be infinitely patient. Wait
each day with a gift. If it mourns or ruminates on the past,

place a long-eared donkey at all times beside it. A donkey
is the best helpmate and companion to your bruised heart.

Day in and day out together they seek the shade, they eat.

One morning they attempt a gentle trot around the enclosure.

The heart is the smaller cousin of the sun, says Joy.
Does it feel heavy? Is it panicky, bucking under your shirt?
Have patience. Your heart is at home in your chest; let it rest there.

The burning you feel is not hatred of your enemies;
not a reaction to eating too many chilis; not the planet
warming, though all those things are there. The burning you feel

is your knowledge of everything: your momentous life.
Your heat, your heart: it all means you mean something,
it makes you make meaning. If it hurts, be still a while:

your heart galloping, panting like a herd of wild horses.

MOTHERHOOD: A MAP

You are here: abject, bereft, clear (all-seeing, also
see-through); disheveled. Euphoric, enervated, flushed, faint,
fierce, and also, generous, gushing milk and patience,
goddess-like, even while grieving—what?—your good, distant self.
Heavy, heaving. Helper; holder of hands or heads.
You'll appear, to some idiots, indignant, indigent, icky.

You'll ignore cries, which is not to say you won't hear them,
no, your rabbit-ears will make you jumpy, jealous
of the free world. Animaled, you'll grow keen, willing
to kill, almost, kept in the kennel of loving a small helpless thing
so helplessly that you'd carry your cub, kindred, *kinder*
through the streets in your very teeth. Kidded: a dual citizen,

luscious and landbound i.e. mother i.e. never *not*.
Owned. Over-committed, overwhelmed, overcome.
Proud, put-upon, pissed off. Playful, prodding, plotting, quiet.
Quaint. Queer. Really reduced, repetitive, regulated
by needs not your own. And yeah, radiant sometimes. Smitten,
sticky. Sated, stressed. Saintly, severe. Tired, tired,

tired, tired, tired, texting too much, teary, your best friend
far away on the other end of the line, she's been through
the trial-by-fire too, and you'd like to call yourselves
triumphant but there's no real teleology here. You're upside-down,
underneath, undone. Vexed, vague, various. You are a *we*,
wived, weaponized, wizened, undeniably witchy.

Wondrous. Aren't you exhausted, being always on exhibit,
extra-human, exiled? Yawn, yowl, yelp. And yet.
Zip up, zone out, zero in, yes, you're zonked but you're also
the ziggurat, juggernaut, zero-sum zig zag. You vibrate,
turn Zohar, azure, zenith. Magicked, you toss missives
through the hedges of yourself: amazed, a maze.

THE JADE CICADA

Folded wings over your stone thorax,
seafoam-shade polished stuff, in a shop
I have never set foot in before today,

an old man tells me your meaning: rebirth.
He ties you on a silk cord, bids me farewell,
and retires, beginning a new life, free

of these old *boddhisattvas*, the slim
goddess Kuanyin, and a fat mahogany
baby foot that keeps one from being

too greedy. Stone bug, you make no summertime
hum, quiet in your yellow zipped pouch.
You are a gift for my beloved on the eve

of his hard-won promotion: lift from him
his headaches, the pain in his right eye,
and let him forget the slights of stupid people

as he retires from the underground labors
of the powerless. Who knows how that feels
better than you, jade cicada? So show us

how your wings sing, rough cry when the cycle
comes around and you climb out, the sun
rising over a ploughed field, green sprouts

breaking through rich soil: you emerge
after seventeen long years like some
divinity! Now you live by drinking the dew.

THE EMPEROR JAHANGIR AT VAH GARDEN

vah [or *wah*], *interj. 1. splendid! wonderful! 2. goodness!*
(expressing astonishment, displeasure, or regret).
—Oxford Hindi-English Dictionary

An artificial lake full of fat, shining fish: the emperor
was en route from Kashmir to Kabul when he stopped here. A rest

between conquests. In the net they came up open-mouthed, fighting air—
"*vah, vah,*" breath-syllable that sounds like a gasp, expressive of

wonder, their small suffering incidental—Jahangir, World-Conqueror,
ordered the servants to mark his catch. One by one: through each fish's

nose they threaded a pearl, and quick while the body still
thrashed a bit, they threw it back—satisfying

plop—and said again, wish astonishment or pleasure
or perhaps with regret, "*Vah,*" and watched as it hung there,

disoriented, then turned its heavy
bejeweled head and swam down, silvery, indistinct

as a face across a hazy battlefield:
first the moon, then the empty night sky.

THE FIRST PERSON

One day she appears: the first person
    you ever made. The circle that you were learning to draw
        now closes, and you take your left hand, then your right, and you

open the first person's eyes, make the slight
    curve of the mouth, scribble-halo of hair, and two things
        you call cheeks, out beyond where the ears usually go.

Nose afterthought. Downward line is a body? No,
    a chest, you say. Arms legs feet extend from it, and she's
        finished. You have made your first person. This one is happy, you say.

Then you make another that is sad. Your first day
    of making people and already you know, there are both.
        You know someone already inside of whom is another

someone, scheduled to emerge in mere months, and by then
    you will have made and discarded multitudes,
        their eyelashes and bellybuttons appearing, disappearing,

their cheeks coming into their faces like
    ordinary cheeks—it will happen, eventually.
        Even now, your future line-drawn army waits,

civilized, in the wings of your brain. They shift from one
    straight leg to the other, impatient, bored, as your first person
        moves across a bare stage, O crooked ecstatic dance.

NOT-YET-OFFICIAL GIRL SCOUT BADGES

Forgetting to Eat Breakfast While Reading Badge
Lazing in Bed on Sunday Morning Badge
Catching Lizards That Got Inside and Releasing Them Badge
Supermarket Dancing Badge
Empathy for the Dog You Hear Howling Every Morning Badge
Boredom Badge
Patience While Your Little Sister Has Another Fit Badge
Badge for Intensity of Focus
Steadfast Refusal to Eat Food You Don't Like Badge
Distractibility Badge (also called Noticing That Flower Badge)
Badge for Laughing So Hard You Fall on the Floor
Rolling Eyes and Returning to Book When Parents Give Educational Lectures Badge
Living in Your Body Badge
Tripping and Falling Badge
Insisting on Your Own Pronunciation of "Mesopotamia" Badge
Comic Book World Creation Badge
Actual World Creation Badge
Bedroom Door Slam Badge
Desiring Justice Badge
Badge of Being Nervous Before the Piano Recital
Badge of Doing It Anyway
Sharing Dad's Obsession with the Pan-Asian Mega-Buffet in Ontario Badge
Secretive Looking Happily in the Mirror Sometimes Badge
Sitting in Mom's Office After School Because She Missed Extended Day Signups and Instead of
      Complaining Putting All Her Paperclips into One Giant Paperclip Chain Badge
Badge of Wonder
Badge of Rage
Not Caring Much About Badges Badge
Born Just Before a Snowstorm Badge
Being Oh Being Beloved Badge

THE WOMAN IN DEGAS' *WOMEN IRONING* LEANS IN

and suddenly it's clear. Not the layers of tulle, not the lightness
of dancers on the stage. Not even the painter's many shades

of small-mindedness: misogynist. Anti-Semite. Voyeur.
No, I see it now: he's painting effort, he's *showing*

the work. Sweat-haloed in a close room
dragging a burning hunk of metal around.

Or else spinning in a cold studio, the arm
stretched *further* to make that long line

that means beauty; the leg *in extremis*, in turnout;
the foot permanently bruised. It's not pretty.

The white linens don't lie that way naturally.
They have to be pummeled, flattened on the table.

*

Beside the sculpted dancer: sculpted racehorse.
Beside the woman ironing: gilded frame, unwrinkled

museum wall. In the painter, the same terror of failure
as in the laundress, the dancer, the horses running

for their lives. The painter alone got, for his effort,
immortality. I wish I couldn't see his utter success.

*

It's the truth: how they massage the tender arches of their feet.
They must soothe themselves; no one else will do it.

Why now, when the endless poster
reproductions, ubiquitous, faded, invisible?

Because I had you, my daughters. Grew you in my body
and pushed you out. Kept you close as my own limbs.

I am at the museum with my mother. In plain sight: our secret
muscles. Our aching lower backs. Our all-seeing eyes.

MICROSCOPIC JAZZ MANDALA

You go to my head… —as sung by Billie Holiday

Under the loupe   enlarged about

    sixteen times   you see your own

furrowed surface: bunched, craggy terrain

    more lunar   than human,

the brain is   like this too, beneath

    the brow, but   hush now, don't

explain, the song   goes, these

    rows of small   mountain ranges

are not the   neurotic kind, they

    mind the curl   of the thumb, they

knuckle punch   and run—oh, but one gets

    exhausted,   body

and soul,   and whose hands

    aren't tired   of being

reasonable　　　　　even Billie, elegantly

　　　armed with that　　white gardenia

in her hair, when　strip-searched

　　　on a drug raid　　in a rage

stood before the　police, looked

　　　into their eyes　　pissed on the floor

ZOOMORPHIC

In the tenth year, she disappeared.
No warning, the mail uncollected,

the potted plants dying on the front porch
until neighbors rescued them,

phone messages answered with silence.
There were rumors that she settled down

in a rainy climate. Or else near the sea.
It was said that she had mastered the art

of zoomorphic calligraphy, and could write
prayers into lions, poems into hawks,

and the ninety-nine names of God
into the shape of the stork that flies

to the Holy Land. That makes pilgrimage.

MANDALA OF THE LONG-LOST RELATIVES

You make a circle of census records, you tie them
      together with bits of digital crabgrass and look
           at the shape they make. In one part of the circle

is your father, and then his father, appearing in a space
      where nothing used to be. Beside him, sisters and brothers,
           a mother carrying them all from a town called

Mayaguez, at the far western end of Puerto Rico,
      onto a ship, to New York City. You make a bigger circle,
           attaching the ship manifest, and birth and marriage

and death records, the arrangement of persons growing
      larger and more detailed: daisy crown turned centerpiece.
           Earlier ancestors take their places, their names

blinking onto the screen in curling, elegant handwriting,
      the turn of the last century. The streets they lived on
           running like lineages between your great-uncle

and a maid who might also be a great-aunt. Little digital leaves
      have sprouted on the tree you are growing from a twig (and now
           you remember the Rose-of-Sharon branch your mother

planted in the ground and tended as it stayed for years looking
      like a stick, mocked, ignored, then grew tall, bloomed). One leaf
           has a message inscribed on it from your distant cousin,

child of the child of your father's uncle. You gather
        more crabgrass and fasten your circle, now a small city
                of mysteries, to your cousin's circle. Thus, you can see the names

not only of the dead, but also the names of the living.

APOLLO

For K.H.

Their voices come back to us thin with static:
describing a pockmarked dustscape, they sound

almost disappointed, until they turn and see—
blue-marbled, strange, familiar—earth

rising over that dry horizon, the continents
all in their right places, clouds

over the Canaries, clear sky over Mexico,
the sea around the land around the sea.

It's Christmas. The astronauts read Genesis
over the airwaves to the listening world,

*And in the beginning God created the heavens
and the earth*, tenderly, with a Texan twang,

as travelers, having crossed oceans, stand on a cliff
squinting into the distance, trying to see home.

AFTERLIFE

Agar firdaus bar roo-e zamin ast,
hamin ast-o hamin ast-o hamin ast.
        —couplet by Amir Khusrao, inscribed on the tomb of Babur in Kabul

If there is a paradise

we arrived, as if at the far bank
of a river, and sat on a cool verandah
upstairs among leaves and
more shady leaves

                    on earth,

it's not mango season, they keep telling us,
so I settle for *mosambi*, sweet lime, for now,
every day I drink half, leave the rest
for you to finish

It is this,

our hotel used to be a *haveli*; the family
still lives in one wing, the women
veiled like proper Rajputs, like
ghosts, sweeping the courtyard

                it is this,

we have no family here, observe no holidays,
and I have given up my phone. Our
old life back home takes on the warm
glow, the softened edges of myth

it is this.

you say you don't like graveyards, tombs,
even beautiful ones, but here we walk
among them and you in a cloud of parakeets
forget about death

BLOOM

Hesperoyucca Whipplei, also known as Our Lord's Candle, Spanish Dagger,
Spanish Bayonet, Quixote Yucca, Chapparal Yucca, Foothill Yucca

Glimpsed from the freeway, and then in the empty lot
off Foothill Boulevard, that blank stretch between
a sex shop and a sushi restaurant: creamy lime-white
stalks of bell-blossoms shoot up eight—no, ten feet
from the spiked primeval sphere of the yucca plant.
Last week they were NOT, neither by the side of the road
nor in my universe, they *did not exist*, and now,
wild, oversized dinosaur flowers, overload
of beauty, I am driving and there is one, and another,
and two or three others, and where can I park and see
them up close? I need to stand beside their insane
height to see my own scale, to let it hit me,
      as a gold rush pioneer, sun-blind, dust-swirled,
      poses for a slow exposure in a weird new world.

THE NEW MOTHER BEFORE THE END TIMES
California

After the rain, how good it is to walk out and feel
the sun on your shoulders! The baby in her stroller

chattering in protest, then asleep. The grey-green olive trees
shine wetly, the silver-grey eucalyptus trees are a scent

you walk through on Mills Avenue carrying with you the knowledge
that around the corner is a tree with a hundred figs

just beginning to ripen. How good to be somewhere still
new to you, to crunch fried sardines in the Filipino supermarket

on a good day, a day when you did not say that terrible thing
to your sister, when you did not stand where a great sharp palm frond

fell with a crash, when you did not show up late for your own
public talk. You have hung the hammock that you bought

in Mexico ten years ago, the one you've been carrying in a box
from one rented apartment to the next, from state to state to state—

you have taken it from the box and thrown the box away
and hung the hammock up with some strange bright orange

nylon tie-down straps you found at the hardware store, and it looks
pretty stupid, honestly, but when you lie in it you can still see

the insanely blue sky and the edge of that fig tree. It is not yet that time
when you will be afraid to let your husband, a citizen, leave the country,

when irrational fears will become reasonable ones. You haven't yet begun
to consider the risks and benefits of certain ordinary acts, certain statements.

The baby's teeth not yet emerged from her gums, the air sweet on your two bodies.
Today you think, briefly, that you might be just the person to give yourself

advice on how to live, though you are under-qualified at best, and at worst
you might be giving yourself some kind of carpal tunnel, holding the baby

at that odd angle all the time, clutching at something else with your free hand.

VOLCANO

No mountaintop
No forest retreat
No cave, no lions bearing witness

You were born into this body
Not by accident
If you're going to have a revelation

Let it be here on the living room floor
With Saafia, who has gotten a piece of paper
And with her blue safety scissors

Cuts out a door in the shape
Of a volcano
She says, I'm going to make the volcano disappear!

No holy orders
No bodhisattva vow
No ascetic regimen

She opens the door—

NOTES

"Babur at Agra": Babur (1438-1530 CE) was the founder of the Mughal dynasty that ruled North India for centuries. His memoir, the *Baburnama*, records, among other things, his longing to return to his homeland in Central Asia. He died in India, and his body was later relocated to Kabul.

"Study Finds" is composed almost entirely of headlines from American news outlets, most from 2019.

"The Last Synagogue in Alexandria": The Jewish community in Alexandria, Egypt, was once in the tens of thousands, but is said to now number less than twenty.

"First Night": Amália Rodrigues (1920-1999) was the most famous modern singer of the Portuguese musical genre *fado* (literally, "fate").

To learn more about Red Bucket Equine Rescue and to donate in support of their mission, please see <https://redbucketrescue.org>

"Zoomorphic": The calligraphic representation of animals is a longstanding tradition in Arabic, Persian and Urdu calligraphy, going back at least to the 15th century.

"Apollo": A recording of the astronauts of Apollo 8 reading from Genesis can be found here: <https:// en.wikipedia.org/wiki/Apollo_8_Genesis_ reading>

ABOUT THE AUTHOR

Chloe Martinez is a poet and scholar of South Asian religions. She is the author of *Corner Shrine* (Backbone Press, 2020), which won the 2019 Backbone Press Chapbook Competition. A former Mellon Mays Fellow and Holden Scholar, her poems have appeared in *Ploughshares*, *Prairie Schooner*, *Shenandoah*, *The Common*, *Waxwing*, and elsewhere. She lives in Claremont, CA, with her husband and two daughters.

ABOUT THE WORD WORKS

Since its founding in 1974, The Word Works has steadily published volumes of contemporary poetry and presented public programs. Its imprints include The Washington Prize, The Tenth Gate Prize, The Hilary Tham Capital Collection, and International Editions.

Monthly, The Word Works offers free literary programs in the Chevy Chase, MD, Café Muse series, and each summer it holds free poetry programs in Washington, D. C.'s Rock Creek Park.

As a 501(c)3 organization, The Word Works has received awards from the National Endowment for the Arts, the National Endowment for the Humanities, the D.C. Commission on the Arts & Humanities, the Witter Bynner Foundation, Poets & Writers, The Writer's Center, Bell Atlantic, the David G. Taft Foundation, and others, including many generous private patrons.

An archive of artistic and administrative materials in the Washington Writing Archive is housed in the George Washington University Gelman Library. The Word Works is a member of the Community of Literary Magazines and Presses and its books are distributed by Small Press Distribution.

wordworksbooks.org

OTHER WORD WORKS BOOKS

Annik Adey-Babinski, *Okay Cool No Smoking Love Pony*
Karren L. Alenier, *Wandering on the Outside*
Andrea Carter Brown, *September 12*
Christopher Bursk, ed., *Cool Fire*
Willa Carroll, *Nerve Chorus*
Grace Cavalieri, *Creature Comforts*
Abby Chew, *A Bear Approaches from the Sky*
Nadia Colburn, *The High Shelf*
Henry Crawford, *Binary Planet*
Barbara Goldberg, *Berta Broadfoot and Pepin the Short // Breaking & Entering: New and Selected Poems*
Akua Lezli Hope, *Them Gone*
Frannie Lindsay, *If Mercy*
Elaine Magarrell, *The Madness of Chefs*
Marilyn McCabe, *Glass Factory*
Kevin McLellan, *Ornitheology*
JoAnne McFarland, *Identifying the Body*
Leslie McGrath, *Feminists Are Passing from Our Lives*
Anatoly Molotkov, *Future Symptoms*
Ann Pelletier, *Letter That Never*
Ayaz Pirani, *Happy You Are Here*
W.T. Pfefferle, *My Coolest Shirt*
Robert Sargent, *Aspects of a Southern Story // A Woman from Memphis*
Julia Story, *Spinster for Hire*
Cheryl Clark Vermeulen, *They Can Take It Out*
Julie Marie Wade, *Skirted*
Miles Waggener, *Superstition Freeway*
Fritz Ward, *Tsunami Diorama*
Camille-Yvette Welsh, *The Four Ugliest Children in Christendom*
Amber West, *Hen & God*
Maceo Whitaker, *Narco Farm*
Nancy White, ed., *Word for Word*